MW01204344

Meditations Along the Taum Sauk Trail

Edgar J. St. Clair

xulon PRESS

ACKNOWLEDGEMENT

This book is lovingly dedicated to my beloved wife, Eva, who has loved me, stood steadfastly beside me and believed in me for the past sixty-three years.

It is also dedicated to the memory of my dear mother, who, over eighty years ago, took her infant son (me) to her pastor and said, "I want to dedicate my son to my Lord and Savior, Jesus Christ."

I also want to include in this dedication my daughter, Carol Mancil, who has encouraged me and has spent countless hours typing and helping me put together the manuscript. Without her the book would never have been completed.

Now faith is being sure of
what we hope for and certain
of what we do not see. ----
And without faith it is
impossible to please God,
because anyone who comes
to him must believe that he
exists and that he rewards
those who earnestly seek
him.

Hebrews 11:1, 6 NIV

TABLE OF CONTENTS

TABLE OF PICTURES.. 6
FOREWORD... 7
"...UNTO THE HILLS...".. 11
THE STONES WEPT... 15
DEVIL'S TOLLGATE 19
"WHAT'S IN A NAME?"... 25
LORD OF THE VALLEYS.. 31
MIRACLE OF THE SEASONS... 35
ALL NATURE REJOICING 37
OLD PATHS... 41
SPRINGS IN THE VALLEYS.. 45
RAINBOW, SYMBOL OF HOPE 49
"WHAT IS MAN, THAT THOU ART MINDFUL OF HIM" 53
"DON'T WAIT TOO LONG" 57
THREE GREAT PARADOXES 61
WITH WINGS AS EAGLES 69
LAYING OUT THE FLEECE 73
FROM TRASH HEAP TO TEMPLE 79
GOD, SPARROWS, AND ME 85
MY SOUL THIRSTETH AFTER THEE, O GOD..................................... 89
MUSHROOMS AND TOADSTOOLS.. 95
I SAW JESUS... 101
UNSEEN ANGELS 109
BUTTERFLIES, SYMBOL OF THE RESURRECTION 115
FREE AT LAST 119
MY TRIBUTE TO THE FIRST BAPTIST CHURCH
        OF SENATH - 1986 126
HOMECOMINGS 135
INDEX OF SCRIPTURES 154
ABOUT THE AUTHOR... 154
REFERENCES.. 155

TABLE OF PICTURES

1 - Johnson Shut-Ins 10
2 - Mina Sauk Falls 14
3 - Devil's Tollgate... 18
4 - Spider Wort 24
5 - Arcadia Valley... 30
6 - Snow & Ice On Trees 34
7 - Arcadia Valley.. 36
8 - Path In Woods 40
9 - Spring In Side Of Hill... 44
10 - Broken Rainbow 48
11 - Starry Sky... 52
12 - Ed St. Clair, My Father... 56
13 - Lindenwood Baptist Church, St. Louis, MO 60
14 - Eagle In Flight 68
15 - Rose Sparkling With Dew 72
16 - Pine Forest... 78
17 - Sparrow 84
18 - Deer In Stream.. 88
19 - Mushrooms 94
20 - Hands.. 100
21 - Angel With Car 108
22 - Butterflies 114
23 - Wappapella School Building, Lowdnes, MO 118
24 - United Methodist Church, Lowdnes, MO 124
25 - First Baptist Church, Senath, MO 126
26 - Ed And Cora St. Clair With Son, Ed Jr. 134
27 - Taum Sauk Lake... 140
28 - Log In Woods... 144

FOREWORD

I was in my late forties when I was diagnosed with arteriosclerosis. On the advice of my cardiologist, I semi-retired to the Arcadia Valley, where I spent many hours literally walking for my life. Over these intervening thirty-five years, my condition has gone through many stages, some promising and others life threatening; from two open heart by-pass surgeries, countless heart catherterizations, three severe heart attacks and three cardiac arrests. (Obviously, Code Blue teams/were able to resuscitate me each time.)

In these pages, I wish to share with my readers some of the sights, sounds, and meditationary thoughts experienced on these long and solitary treks. My intentions have been good; but it was only as I recently read and prayed Bruce Wilkinson's The Prayer of Jabez, that God has answered my prayer, blessed me, enlarged my territory, kept His hand upon me and delivered me from evil that I should cause no pain. Now, I fervently pray that he may work through these enlarged ministry opportunities to point the way to relief for the hurting and peace to troubled hearts.

In recent months, I have been found to have a lymphoma cancer on my spine, and the Prayer of Jabez has taken on a significance and urgency not felt previously. Now, confined to my home, I am reduced to dependency on notes made, a journal sometimes kept and a memory still good into my eighty-second year. But, like the Apostle Paul, "*I can do all things through Christ who strengthens me.*" (Philippians 4:13) These meditations come from that deep well of experience and memory.

> Create in me a pure heart, O God, and renew a steadfast spirit within me.
> Psalm 51:10 niv

In the same way, the Spirit
helps us in our weakness.
We do not know what we
ought to pray for, but the
Spirit himself intercedes for
us with groans that words
cannot express.
Romans 8:26 NIV

A sparkling stream meanders across the valley to go rushing out through the "shut-ins" as though in a hurry to reach the sea.

"...UNTO THE HILLS..."

There's a lovely valley nestled among the green clad hills of Missouri on which God must have lavished special loving attention at creation. Springs abound among the lush green pasture lands, and a sparkling stream meanders across its breadth to go rushing out through the "shut-ins" as though in a hurry to reach the sea.

Long ago someone named this valley, "Arcadia." Taken from the name of a pastoral district of the Peloponnesus of ancient Greece, the term today is defined as: "any place of rural peace and simplicity." How appropriate! How fitting a name—Arcadia Valley.

Rising above this valley on the south like a sentinel stands the highest point of land in all the state, Taum Sauk Mountain. A trail first followed by the moccasin-clad feet of old Taum Sauk's warrior-hunters, winds its way down the valley, over Shepherd Mountain, and up the hardwood-clad slopes of Taum Sauk. It is the inspiration that I received as I, too, followed this age-old trail that I want to share in these pages.

I first saw Arcadia Valley in 1942. Struck dumb by its beauty, I silently vowed to some day come back. And come back I did, though many years later. Struck down by heart disease, I came to this peaceful valley to find quiet and peace, and to give my stress ravaged body a chance to recover. So it was that I began to spend many hours in the solitude I found along the Taum Sauk Trail and other by-ways around the valley. As I lifted my eyes to the towering hills surrounding me (Pilot Knob, Shepherd, Taum Sauk, Arcadia Heights) my heart thrilled as must have the heart of the Sweet Psalmist of Israel, David, when he said: *"I will lift up mine eyes unto the hills from whence cometh my help; my help cometh from the Lord who made Heaven and Earth."* (Psalms 121:1)

I knew somehow that here in the peace and solitude of these eternal hills I would find the help I needed. It came, as the bitterness and self-pity that I had wallowed in flowed out of me. In their place came a peace and tranquillity that I had thought was gone forever. And the refrain of the old gospel song took on new meaning for me: "There'll be peace in the valley, for me….."

> I thank Christ Jesus our Lord, who has given me strength, that he considered me faithful, appointing me to His service.
> I Timothy 1:12 NIV

2

A lovely little waterfall called, Mina Sauk Falls, is a lovely
spot visited by many hikers.

THE STONES WEPT

About a mile down the Taum Sauk Trail from the lookout tower and picnic area on the summit of Taum Sauk Mountain is a lovely little waterfall called the Mina Sauk Falls, where a small watercourse plunges over a high granite ledge. It is a lovely spot visited and photographed by many hikers.

Perhaps the greatest attraction of the falls is the legend that is attached to it. How and when this story began no one knows, but it has been told and retold for so long that it has truly become a legend and has gained some authenticity. Here in brief form is how it goes.

Many, many years ago, before any white man came to inhabit this section of the Ozarks, a sub-tribe of the Osage Indians lived here, led by a great and powerful chief named Taum Sauk. Their main village, which was situated on the summit of the highest point in what is now the State of Missouri still, bears the chief's name. Taum Sauk's warrior-hunters roamed the surrounding hills and valleys and took a rich harvest from the abundant game of the forest and the fish that filled the streams.

The chief had a beautiful daughter, Mina Sauk, who was his pride and joy. Many a fine brave looked on her with adoration and dreamed of claiming her as his bride.

One day, returning from a raid on an enemy tribe, the chief brought a young enemy brave which he had taken captive. A chief's son, he was proud and handsome. He soon won the heart of Mina Sauk, and in turn succumbed to her maidenly charms. Their love grew, in spite of the opposition of Taum Sauk, and soon they were asking to be married. Refused, they attempted to flee, only to be captured and returned. The young brave was executed. This was done by casting him over a cliff, to die on the rocks below. Mina Sauk, in her grief, threw herself over the cliff to her death on the rocks beside the broken body of her beloved. The tragedy was so sad that even the granite rocks wept and formed the falls that still bear the name of the star-crossed princess.

Often on my walks, I have taken the trail down to the falls and back. Often I have thought of that little story, sad and poignant. Whether it has any truth to it or not, it illustrates the hard-heartedness and innate cruelty that we see so often in people—hearts even harder than the red granite bedrock of these ancient hills. I am reminded of how God has said that if we will but trust Him, He will take away our hearts of stone and give us instead a tender heart of flesh.

The daily news often chronicles the hard-hearted deeds of people. Many terrible crimes are perpetrated daily that bring suffering, heartache, and despair to God's children. We hear these things and wonder how anyone can be so cruel and hard-hearted. I look at lovely Mina Sauk Falls and imagine the red granite stones weeping today for the tragedies happening all about us. I pray that the gentle heart of Jesus may touch the lives of multitudes and replace their stony hearts with hearts of compassion and love.

Thank you, Lord, for loving me, even when my heart was cold and hard against you. I thank you, too, for giving me a new heart to care for others. Thank you, Lord, for the lessons learned along my Taum Sauk Trail.

3

To Native Americans a footpath, to pioneers a saddle trail, and to early settlers a wagon road, this landmark became known as "The Devil's Tollgate."

DEVIL'S TOLLGATE

About a mile after leaving Mina Sauk Falls, one hiking the Taum Sauk Trail comes to another awe inspiring natural phenomenon. A mammoth red granite monolith was thrust above the earth's surface by some prehistoric upheaval of the earth's crust, or else was exposed by centuries of water and wind erosion. Some force, beyond the ken of mere mortals, has split this huge stone as a housewife cleaves a layer cake. The two walls thus formed, rising sheer some thirty feet in height, were moved apart, leaving a passage about eight feet wide between. To Native Americans a foot path, to pioneers a saddle trail, and to early settlers a wagon road, this landmark became known as "The Devil's Tollgate."

Although well worth the effort, one must pay a price in expenditure of energy to view this sight. For myself, it took years of waiting and longing before I felt capable of the four mile round trip down the trail and back, the return all upgrade. When finally made, I found the sight well worth the cost, though it is aptly called a "tollgate."

As I have pondered the experience, it is the name that has intrigued me. A few lines from a poem read while in school comes to mind: "They say that life is a highway, and the milestones are the years; and now and then there's a tollgate where you buy your way with tears." Surely, most of us can look back at the way we have come and remember vividly the many "tollgates" through which we have passed, paying for our passage with tears. We must remember how Jesus said of the gates and the ways:

> *"Wide is the gate and easy the way that leads to destruction, and many there be which go in thereat; because strait is the gate and narrow the way that leads to life, and few there are that find it."* (Matthew 7:13-14)

I have found that very few worthwhile things in life come cheap. A corollary is that those things of life that we have paid most dearly for are those that we cherish most. News broadcasts are filled with reports of the swindling of vulnerable folk by unscrupulous con-artists. Preying on those most gullible, these greedy felons offer something for nothing or next to nothing; and their victims fall for the con. This has given rise to the often-repeated warning: "If it seems too good to be true, it probably is." Yes, worthwhile things have their price, and that which seems cheap usually is just that, cheap.

In his Prelude to *THE VISION OF SIR LAUNFEL*, Lowell penned these memorable words:

> *At the Devil's booth all things are sold.*
> *Each ounce of dross costs its ounce of gold.*
> *Baubles we buy with a whole soul's tasking,*
> *While Heaven alone is given away:*
> *'Tis only God may be had for the asking.*[1]

While all we have said is true, and the worthwhile things of life do not come cheap, the most wondrous truth of all is that the most precious possession we have cannot be purchased at any price, but only received as the free gift of God. In Romans 6:23 we read: *"The wages of sin is death, but the gift of God is eternal life through Jesus Christ our Lord."*

Thank you, God, for the gift of your love and for that new and everlasting life in Christ Jesus. Thank you, Father, for not making your way of life cheap or easy, lest we take it for granted. Thank you, too, for the

inspiration I find along my Taum Sauk Trail. In Jesus'
name I pray. Amen.

Cast all your anxiety on him
because he cares for you.
1 Peter 5:7 NIV

> Therefore, I tell you, whatever you ask for in prayer, believe that you have received it, and it will be yours.
>
> **Mark 11:24 NIV**

4

The Spider Wort:
"What's in a name? A rose by any other name would smell
as sweet." - William Shakespeare

"WHAT'S IN A NAME?"

One pleasing feature of the Ozarks is the abundance and variety of wild flowers, and the Taum Sauk Trail is no exception. From spring through autumn I was delighted daily with beautiful flowers that would have challenged the brush and palette of the most gifted artist, but disappointed that I knew so few of them by name. A <u>Field-Guide to Missouri Wild Flowers</u> became a necessary and often used companion on my walks. Soon the desire to capture these beautiful objects for future enjoyment led me to add a 35mm camera to my gear.

One morning, my attention was caught by a glimpse of delicate lavender among the dry leaves collected beneath a low branching post oak shrub. Getting on my knees, I carefully parted the leaves to expose a lovely three-petaled lavender flower. The color and texture were exquisite. I adjusted my camera settings and photographed this rare and delicate beauty whose identity was still unknown to me.

My efforts to identify the flower were in vain for several days. Finally, after receiving the developed and printed film, I found my treasure and learned its name.   I had discovered and photographed a blossoming Spider Wort or a Spider Lily.

My first reaction to the name was one of disappointment. The flower was so pretty that I had somehow expected it to have an equally pretty name. But Spider WORT! Ugh! The name just didn't fit. Why not a name more descriptive of the delicately beautiful blossom? Why not Lavender Lily, or maybe, Lavender Trefoil? I thought of other beautiful flowers, not nearly so lovely, with more appealing names: Sweet Williams, Lady's Slipper, or Primrose.

However, what was it that the "Bard of Avon" has said about a name? "What's in a name? A rose by any other name would smell as sweet." Of course! It isn't the name that makes the flower, but the flower that gives meaning and beauty to the name. The rose came first; and when named, forever gives a lovely and fragrant connotation to the name, "Rose."

As I continued to ponder this subject, the answer came through to me, clear and satisfying. I realized that it all had to do with the Creator. Had not

God made the flower while man had made the name? When God had finished His creation, He looked at it and saw that it was very good. Even the forbidden fruit that Satan used to beguile Eve was pleasing to the eye. Without man's interference, there would have been no ugliness anywhere. God had made the lovely blossom to bloom there in the obscure place and gladden the eye of this lonely hiker with beauty; man had created the unattractive name.

The poet, Joyce Kilmer, expressed something of this sentiment in *TREES*:

> *Poems are made by fools like me,*
> *But only God can make a tree.*[2]

So, from now on, whenever I hear an ugly epithet laid on any of God's creatures, be it herb, beast or man, I will remember the lesson learned from the Spider Wort along my Taum Sauk Trail and rejoice over my encounter with it there.

I will be reminded, too, of the words of another poet, Emerson, who wrote of a similar experience in his *RHODORA:*

> *Why you were there, O rival of the rose,*
> *I never tho't to ask; I never knew.*[3]

But in my simple ignorance suppose
The self-same power that brought me there,
brought you." [3]

So I go on trudging my solitary way along the Taum Sauk Trail, daily being assured that God in His providence does not do anything nor permit anything without a purpose, and that all the purposes of God are benevolent.

"For all things work together for good to them that love God..." (Romans 8:28)

Delight yourself in the Lord
and he will give you the
desires of your heart.
Psalms 37:4 NIV

I have been crucified with Christ and I no longer live, but Christ lives in me. The life I live in the body, I live by faith in the Son of God, who loved me and gave himself for me.

Galatians 2:20 NIV

5

Arcadia Valley
"…a breathtaking vista.. beautiful to behold…"

LORD OF THE VALLEYS

From a scenic overlook built by the park service near the summit of Taum Sauk Mountain, one can look out over the major portion of Arcadia Valley. It is a breath-taking vista, beautiful to behold. Standing there, awe struck by its beauty, I have mused on the many different meanings the Valley has come to have for me over the many years I have spent there. There I had been blessed serving as pastor and Jesus' under-shepherd of His flock. There I had been part of many victories for Christ. There, too, I had wept over the victories Satan won in the lives of some I had not been able to lead to Christ. There I had known the sorrow and sense of loss in the death of parents, and the mixed tears and rejoicing in the growth to adulthood of our children and their leaving the home nest for lives on their own. Many memories, some sad, others joyous and happy.

There are many references in the Bible to valleys, most of them with very meaningful names. We read of the Valley of Weeping. The Psalmist sings to God:

31

"Blessed are those whose strength is in you, who have set their hearts on pilgrimage. As they pass through the Valley of Baca (weeping) they make it a place of springs..."
(Psalms 84:56 NIV)

What a beautiful thought! All of us have to walk through our own valley of weeping, but for those whose trust and dependency is in the Lord, it becomes as a valley filled with fresh flowing water in an arid land.

In that best-known and beloved Shepherd Psalm, we read of the Valley of the Shadow of Death: *"Even though I walk through the valley of the shadow of death, I will fear no evil, for you are with me..."*(Psalm 23:4 NIV) This refers to those times when we come face to face with the reality of our own mortality. Death is a reality for all of us, every one. *"It is appointed unto men once to die...."* (Hebrews 9:27). Death is a certainty for every one; but if we know Christ, we can face that certainty, walk that valley, without fear because we trust in our Lord's promise: *"Lo, I am with you always, even to the end of the world."* (Matthew 28:20)

As I ponder these truths, I am reminded of another Bible valley, the Valley of Blessing. The twentieth chapter of II Chronicles tells of a great victory God won for Judah over a coalition of three enemies: Moab, Ammon, and Seir. Greatly outnumbered, Judah was not allowed to give battle, but only to 'wait upon God.' The enemy was utterly destroyed, and the people of Judah...."*assembled themselves in the valley of Beracah (blessing); for there they blessed the Lord...*" (II Chronicles 20:26) Realizing that every victory I have had was given to me by my Heavenly Father, neither won nor earned by myself, I must pause again and again in my own Valley of Blessing and praise His Holy Name.

Thank you, my Father, for making my valley of weeping into a place of springs. Thank you, Lord, for helping me walk through my valley of the shadow of death without fear, hand-in-hand with you. For all your blessings, Father, I make this, my valley home, a valley of blessing; forever praising you from the very depth of my soul. Amen.

6

"…evergreens, bowed under their burden of ice, were like weary old men with frost in their whiskers.

MIRACLE OF THE SEASONS

One cold morning I debated whether or not to take a walk. Later, I was glad I did, for my way led me through a veritable fairy wonderland. The freezing mist had coated every shrub and tree with ice until the hardwoods glittered in the sunlight like wealthy dowagers bedecked with jewels; and the evergreens, bowed under their burden of ice, were like weary old men with frost in their whiskers.

For this is February, and the earth still sleeps under her blanket of ice and snow. Soon, however, the soft caress of spring showers and the gentle whisper of warm breezes will awaken her. Then she will stretch herself like a sleepy child awakening from slumber. Buds will burst, flowers bloom, and the birds will sing with the sheer joy of living.

Thank you, dear God, for the miracle of the seasons with their recurrent reminder of the reality of the resurrection, and the constant assurance that you are ever able to make all things new.

7

"I could look out over the tranquil valley, ringed by the green-clad hills that rolled away, fold on fold, as far as my eyes could reach."

ALL NATURE REJOICING

"For ye shall go out with joy and be led forth in peace..."
Isaiah 55:12a

One day my heart was so filled with the joy of walking in the awareness of the presence of Jesus abiding in my heart and the loving watch-care of my Heavenly Father, that I felt it might burst. Finding a comfortable place, I just sat and meditated. It was one of those lovely days when all nature seemed to be in harmony. The sky above was so clear and clean that it looked as though it had been freshly washed and hung out to dry. From where I sat, I could look out across the tranquil valley, ringed by the green-clad hills that rolled away, fold on fold, as far as my eyes could reach. It was one of those soul-satisfying times when you wish there were others there to share and rejoice with you.

I lifted my hands and clapped them in a spontaneous expression of my gladness. I began to pray, aloud, counting my blessings and giving voice to the gratitude that swelled in my breast. With no thought of embarrassment, I began to recite the words of that beautiful hymn popularized by George Beverly Shea, "*HOW GREAT THOU ART."*

> *Oh Lord, my God, When I in awesome wonder,*
> *Consider all the worlds Thy hands have made…*
> *Then sings my soul, my Savior, God, to Thee:*
> *'How great Thou art; How great Thou art'…* [4]

A passage of scripture from that great chapter Isaiah 55:12, came to my mind. Finding the passage in my pocket Bible, I read it again and again.

> *For ye shall go out with joy and be led forth in*
> *peace.*
> *The mountains and the hills shall break forth*
> *into singing,*
> *And all the trees of the field shall clap their*
> *hands.*

Ah, how wonderfully God was fulfilling this promise for me this day. I heard with a new comprehension the rustle of the tree foliage about me as the gentle breeze helped them to "clap their hands;" and all the rolling hills about me seemed to join in singing: "My God, how great Thou art."

I remembered the account by an aged lady member of my church flock of a time when she said she guessed she had shocked her Baptist brothers and sisters by shouting, "right in service. I just couldn't help myself, Pastor. A big chunk of glory just fell on me and I just couldn't keep from rejoicing."

What an apt expression of what I was feeling this day! I cried out of my heart, "Thank you, Lord, for giving me such a wonderful chunk of glory, too. My God, how great Thou art."

> My grace is sufficient for you, for my power is made perfect in weakness. Therefore I will boast all the more gladly about my weaknesses, so that Christ's power may rest on me.
> 2 Corinthians 12:9 niv

8

> *"Stand in the ways and see, and ask for the old paths where is the good way, and walk therein..."*
> Jeremiah 6:16

OLD PATHS

As I walked the Taum Sauk Trail, I became aware of many small side trails diverging from the main trail. As had many others before me, I was tempted to turn aside and explore some of these. I soon learned, however, that they all ended in a jumble of rocks or a briar thicket, where the original explorer had turned back; or else had simply circled back into the main trail further along. Speculating on the origin of these trails that led nowhere, I came to the conclusion that each of them must have had its beginning with a curious hiker who had simply turned aside to explore new terrain, look for an easier route, or to investigate something that had attracted his attention. Others, seeing his diverging tracks turned aside just to see where they led, with each succeeding explorer making the new trail more clearly defined to attract the next curious hiker.

How like the path of life is my Taum Sauk Trail! There is a clearly marked, well defined path for us to follow. However, many diverging paths tempt us to turn aside from the well-marked trail. All of us have succumbed at times to the temptation to turn aside from the known trail to explore the strange, new, enticing by-way, only to come eventually to a dead end in some thorny tangle, or at the brink of some dark and forbidding abyss.

When our straying feet lead us into such difficulties, we have just one sensible course: turn and retrace our steps, back to the straight and narrow, to the known way. How much better, we conclude, to have stayed on the main trail in the first place, and not to have wasted our precious resources of energy and time on a way that led us nowhere.

The Prophet Jeremiah must have observed a similar phenomenon, for he wrote:

Stand in the ways and see, and ask for the old paths where is the good way, and walk therein, and ye shall find rest for your souls. (Jeremiah 6:16)

Come and see what God has done, how awesome his works in man's behalf!

Psalm 66:5 NIV

9

Emerging from the side of the hill was the spring. *"He sendeth the springs into the valleys, which run among the hills. They give drink to every beast of the field..."* Psalms 104:10-11

SPRINGS IN THE VALLEYS

As I have walked the Taum Sauk Trail, in search of strength for my body and peace and serenity for my jaded spirit, I have wavered between hope and despair. Whatever progress I was making was not constant and there seemed to be as many days filled with despair as with hope. Whether I was gaining in health and strength or not, there were many other rewards from my efforts as God spoke to me through almost daily encounters with His creation and His creatures.

One morning, as I plodded along my trail, I came across a tiny little brook, a "hollow branch" in Ozark dialect. The crystal clear water trickled along over the stones, occasionally forming small pools of quiet water, only to spill out of them again to go babbling along on its way to the sea. I was intrigued by this stream, because at this dry season, the hollows should have been dry.

This morning, I turned aside from the trail as some impulse moved me to seek the source of this lovely little stream. Walking was difficult over uneven

45

ground; often impeded by rocks, underbrush, and fallen timbers. Occasionally the stream would disappear, and I would think I had found the spring that gave it birth. Yet each time, I would find a little further on where it had gone underground and could follow it still further. Finally, I came to the "head" of the hollow; and there, emerging from the side of the hill was the spring—a small pool at the base of a great oak tree. Clean gravel gleamed beneath the water. Wild ferns grew profusely all around. Roots of the ancient oak near the water were covered by moss, as were the stones that lined its edge.

Bending low, I drank thirstily from the spring, and then sat back to enjoy the sylvan beauty of the place. I wondered how many of God's creatures had slaked their thirst from these waters as I had. I wondered too how many of God's creatures had felt gratitude for the gift of water, as I had. Of course, dumb animals could neither feel nor express gratitude for God's providential care and provision. How like dumb animals is God's higher creation, man; to take and take of God's bounty, and so seldom contemplate their source in gratitude and love.

"He sendeth the springs into the valleys, which run among the hills. They give drink to every beast of the field..." (Psalm 104:10-11)

May God be gracious to us
and bless us and make his
face shine upon us, that your
ways may be known on
earth, your salvation among
all nations.
Psalm 67:1-2 NIV

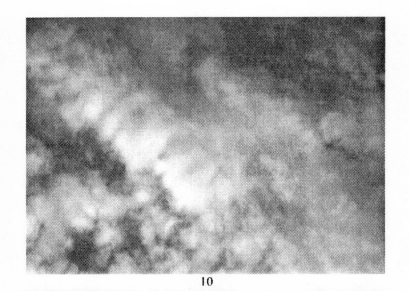

10

A patch of pastel colors appeared in the midst of the clouds.
No arc, no pattern, just patches of rainbow colors

RAINBOW, SYMBOL OF HOPE

The day was dark, and the clouds hung threateningly across a lowering sky. As sometimes happens, my mood was as dark as the sky. As I pondered, a few words from a poem long ago studied in a high school English class formed in my mind: *"Into all lives some rain must fall. Some days must be dark and dreary."*[5]

However, this day, things were different. As I watched, a patch of pastel colors appeared in the midst of the clouds. At first there was just one, then, in another place, another, and another. No arc, no pattern, just patches of rainbow colors. Then a few more words from that long forgotten poem came to me: *"Behind the clouds is the sun, still shining."*[6]

As I watched the scudding clouds and several rainbow hued patches, I realized that they were, actually, parts of a rainbow, broken or partially obscured by the thicker, darker clouds. The comforting thought came to me that the rainbow, symbol of God's promise to Noah, might be broken; but the promise was still true and inviolate. Never in all of man's history has one of God's promises to his children been broken. It was as though God was saying to me: "It's all right, my child, it's all right. I'm still here, and my promises are: *"in me Yea, and in me, Amen.* (II Corinthians 1:20)

Rejoicing in that heaven-sent sign of hope, and uplifted in spirit, I knew that indeed everything is all right. God is not dead! His Son, Jesus, still reigns! The clouds that sometimes dim our vision will, in His own time, be rolled away. Every question will be answered; every longing will be satisfied; and we shall know, even as we are known.

Thank you, God, for your promises to us, and for the reassurances you so graciously provide when we are most in need of them! Amen!

This is the confidence we
have in approaching God:
that if we ask anything
according to his will, he hears
us. And if we know that he
hears us --- whatever we
ask---we know that we have
what we asked of him.
1 John 5:14-15 NIV

11

"How tiny is the planet Earth in the midst of God's creation, and how little I…"

"WHAT IS MAN, THAT THOU ART MINDFUL OF HIM?"

Although my walks along the by-ways of Arcadia Valley were by necessity made by day, there were times when something within led me to stand outside my home and gaze at the beauty and immensity of God's great handiwork in space. Astronomers tell us of our Milky Way Galaxy with its millions of solar systems, with billions of other galaxies beyond that. My mind cannot comprehend the reality of God's infinity, and I can only stand in awe and breathe, "My God, how great thou art;" and with the Psalmist ask: *"What is man that thou art mindful of him?"* (Psalms 8:4)

How tiny is planet earth in the midst of God's creation. How infinitesimally small on this little island in space is each of its billions of human beings. How little I am! Yet in Jeremiah 1:5 God has said that when I was yet only a single microscopic cell, before I was yet conceived in my mother's womb, he knew me. He had a plan and a purpose for my life. Out of the depths of my soul, I cry out, "Oh, God, it is too wonderful for me."

Out of such a time of contemplation and meditation, I penned the following simple little poem:

WONDER
God made the mountains
God made the plains.
God made the sun to shine,
And God sent the rains.
God created all that is,
Space, earth, sky, and sea.
God created every living thing;
So, God created ME!
When God finished creating things,
He rested, and then He stood.
Looking on His handiwork,
He smiled and said, "It's good!"
God loves all He made,
My Bible says to me.
God loves every living soul;
So, GOD LOVES ME!"[7]

What a profound truth, and yet what a simple promise. How humbling and, yes, how exalting to my soul.

Thank you, my God, for loving me; so unlovely, so unloving, and so unlovable. Thank you, Father, for your handiwork in me. A long time ago I prayed:

54

"Have thine own way, Lord; have thine own way. Thou art the potter. I am the clay. Mold me and make me after thy will while I am waiting, yielded and still."[8] Father, I have not always been pliant in thy hands, and I am still an unfinished work. Forgive me, Lord, and beat down all my resistance. Help me to be able to pray with all sincerity: "Thy will be done IN ME." In the precious name of Jesus, thy Son, my Savior. Amen

> "Holy, holy, holy is the Lord Almighty: the whole earth is full of his glory.
> Isaiah 6:3 niv

12

My father in the chair where he closed his last letter to me:
"Don't wait too long…(to visit)."

"DON'T WAIT TOO LONG"

My walks had now become drastically shortened due to my deteriorated heart condition. I thought of the many things I had planned to do, sometime, but had waited for a more convenient or opportune time. Now, it was too late. There was the trip to the Holy Land I had longed to take. I wanted to see the places where Jesus had been, walk the pathways where His sandaled feet had trod, and perhaps feel His blessed presence even more intensively than ever before. I had waited until finances were better, or the political climate was improved, or the demand on my time here was more permissible. Now, I had waited too long.

There were the books I had intended to write, sometime. Some of these had been roughly outlined, but the actual writing had been put off on one excuse or another. Now, time was running out. I had waited too long. Oh, procrastination! You thief of time and opportunity!

I thought of the last letter I received from my father before his death. Although he lived only about one hundred fifty miles from me, the demands of my busy pastorate kept me from visiting him as often as I wished. I had a one-week vacation coming up, and had written him that we would visit sometime during that week. However, I decided we would visit our eldest daughter, recently married and living in Colorado, first, and then visit my father when we came back. To my sorrow, he passed away on our second day in Colorado. He had ended his last letter by saying how he looked forward to our visit, and "Don't wait too long." To my regret, I had.

How many people wait too long in carrying out good intentions? I remember the young wife and mother in my church, depressed and needing counsel, confessing to me how, in her teens, she knew she had been called of God to surrender her life to full-time Christian service. In a tiff with her mother, and out of spite, she had married instead. How sad was her tearful lament: "And now it is too late!"

How many, like Felix, who was almost convinced by the Apostle Paul to believe in Jesus Christ, but decided to *"wait for a more convenient season,"* which never came. (Acts 24:24-26) How important is our Lord's admonition *to "make your (our) calling and election sure,* (II Peter 1:10); and *"today, if you will hear His voice, harden not your heart."* (Psalm 95:7-8)

Oh, God, forgive us for the times we have put off the important for the mundane. Lord, teach us to *"redeem the time,"* so that we may never have to, like King David, *"shed yesterday's tears today."*

> I am not ashamed of the gospel, because it is the power of God for the salvation of everyone who believes.
> Romans 1:16 niv

13

My city church was located on a busy six-lane thoroughfare.
Lindenwood Baptist Church, St. Louis, Missouri

THREE GREAT PARADOXES

My progress during the weeks and months that I have walked my Taum Sauk Trail has been painfully slow and discouraging. Yet today as I rested for a while beneath one of the great oaks that have become familiar old friends to me now, I reflected on the physical and mental torture of those first days of my journey, and I knew that I have made progress.

Physically, I still have a long way to go back to the strength and stamina that had once been my source of pride. Yet how far I have come from those days when only a few steps brought the squeezing chest pains and labored gasping for breath, when the little white nitroglycerin pellets were my constant companions and my tenuous lifeline. My walks are much longer now, and my rest stops fewer. Although I still go nowhere without my little bottle of nitroglycerin tablets, I very seldom have to fumble one out of the bottle and place it under my tongue. Truly, I have made progress.

However, as rewarding as has been my physical progress, I have gained in other and far more satisfying ways. I think Michael Fairless, in his little English classic, *THE ROADMENDER*, has expressed it very well:

> *"Yet I have learnt to understand dimly the truths of three great paradoxes---the blessing of a curse, the voice of silence, and the companionship of solitude."*[9]

It is difficult today to escape the intrusion of noise. My city church was located on a busy six-lane thoroughfare, and the parsonage where we lived was next door. There was a continual din of racing engines, screeching tires, and wailing sirens. From my bed at night or from my study by day, this continual din pervaded every moment of my life. Of necessity my mind and body made some adjustment to it, some psychological tuning out its invasion. Yet it was there, and it had erosive and corrosive effects on my entire being.

However, when I first came to the valley and the quietness of my solitary walks, it was the silence that intruded. My body and mind, long adjusted to the din of the city, had now to adjust to the silence. Like Elijah the Prophet who heard God, not in the storm or wind or earthquake or fire, but in His still small voice from the silence that followed the storm, so He has spoken to me from the silence. The quietness without has accomplished a quieting of the storms that raged within and brought a peace that passes all understanding. Surely, I have come to understand the truth of the paradox of the "voice of silence."

Psychologists tell us that one of the basic in-born fears of people is the fear of being left alone. From the cradle to the grave, people crave the companionship of others. Yet, there is also a basic need in one for some time spent alone with self. Today it has become increasingly more difficult to escape the intrusion of crowds, and find a time and place for solitude. People fill their days with activity in the busy marketplace, and their leisure time in pursuit of pleasure in company of others. Youth fill every moment with the flashing images of television or the deafening rhythms of contemporary music. Here on my trail, I have learned to obey the admonition to *"Be still, and know that I am God..."* (Psalm 46:10)

My son has a beautiful singing talent. When he graduated from high school, his classmates and teachers asked him to sing at the commencement exercises. He chose for his two numbers, *CLIMB EVERY MOUNTAIN*, from THE SOUND OF MUSIC, and *I'LL NEVER WALK ALONE*. In memory I can still hear his youthful voice ringing out those words of faith. During my solitary walks, I have more than ever come to understand their meaning, for I have truly come to understand the truth of the paradox of the "companionship of solitude." In the solitude of my walks, I have never been lonely, for I have felt a presence and a companionship that also passes all understanding.

Perhaps most important of all has been the change in my perception of my physical disability. My initial reaction was one of bitterness and rebellion. The bitter question, "Why?" was continually in my mind and often on my lips. As the quiet and peace has brought some measure of healing to my body, so it has to my spirit; and I can feel a kindred spirit and understanding with Joseph, son of Jacob. His brothers hated him, conspired to murder him, and sold him into slavery. Potiphar's wife tried vainly to seduce him, lied about him, and had him imprisoned. Finally, the King's butler forgot Joseph's kindness and his own promise, and left Joseph languishing in prison. However, God vindicated His actions, and when Joseph was reunited with his brothers, he could say, *"You meant it for evil, but God meant it for good."* (Genesis 50:20).

Job, deprived and afflicted beyond human endurance, still trusted God. God vindicated his faith and blessed him "more in the end than He had in the beginning." The Apostle Paul sought release from his own "thorn in the flesh," but through it came to know God's all-sufficient grace.

Pondering these truths, the last of bitterness and self-pity drained out of me. At last I could fall on my knees there on my solitary trail and thank God for the blessing of my affliction and truly believe His promise that *"all things work together for good to them that love God."* (Romans 8:28) For I had "learnt to understand dimly the truths of three great paradoxes, the blessing of a curse, the voice of silence, and the companionship of solitude."[9]

I have told you these things, so that in me you may have peace. In this world you will have trouble. But take heart! I have overcome the world.
John 16:3 niv

To him who is able to keep
you from falling and to
present you before his
glorious presence without
fault and with great joy ---
to the only God our Savior be
glory, majesty, power and
authority, through Jesus
Christ our Lord, before all
ages, now and forevermore!
Amen

Jude 1:24-niv

14

"*...they that wait upon the Lord shall renew their strength;
they shall mount up with wings as eagles.*" Isaiah 40:31

WITH WINGS AS EAGLES

As I walked the Taum Sauk Trail, so feebly and haltingly at first, I was almost daily rewarded with encounters with wondrous and meaningful things that previously had gone unnoticed or taken for granted. Now I seemed to have a newly awakened awareness and appreciation for things that were no longer commonplace.

One particular morning I was especially depressed and discouraged. I was so very weak, and the least exertion brought on the dreaded and frightening chest pains, so that I was only able to walk very short distances between rest stops. Wallowing in self-pity, discouraged to the point of giving up, I dropped wearily on the ground and leaned back against a tree. The azure sky above me was so clear that one could see forever, and for long moments I was lost in its infinitude.

How long I sat there I do not know, but finally my eyes began to focus on a distant speck in the vast emptiness of the sky. For some reason, beyond reason, I couldn't take my eyes from this object so distant as to be beyond identification. Making ever widening circles; it dropped lower and lower, until I knew that it was some large bird. Wheeling and turning on out-stretched wings, it sought out and rode the thermal currents. Occasionally, when the up-drafts were lost, it beat those great wings and climbed until it again found the supporting currents, when it would again soar, strong and carefree above the mountaintops. As it banked, light reflected off its snow-white crest and tail pinions, and I knew that I was watching the flight of a bald eagle, the most majestic of birds.

Inspired, I took my little Bible out of my pocket and began to hunt a scripture long forgotten. Miraculously, I found it almost immediately, and the words seemed to leap from the pages.

> *He giveth power to the faint; and to them that have no might He increaseth strength. Even the youths shall faint and be weary, and the young men shall utterly fall: But they that wait upon the Lord shall renew their strength; they shall mount up with wings as eagles; they shall run, and not be weary; they shall walk, and not faint.*
> (Isaiah 40:29-31)

My heart surged within my breast, and tears filled my eyes. Somehow I had run ahead of God in my headstrong way, and now I was faint and weary on that way, but here was His promise; here was the way. I must wait upon the Lord that my strength might be renewed.

O Lord, give me patience and faith to wait upon you, that in your own good time, in your own way, I may receive renewed strength, that I may again run without weariness and walk without fainting.

Amen! Praise and glory and wisdom and thanks and honor and power and strength be to our God forever and ever. Amen!.
Revelation 7:12 niv

15

"Dewdrops glittered as the sun's rays were diffused
through them…"

LAYING OUT THE FLEECE

Early one morning as I began my daily walk, I was attracted by the huge amount of dew that had fallen the night before. Grass and shrubs were soaked with it, and it dripped in profusion from the tree foliage. Dewdrops glittered as the sun's rays were diffused through them. The sight set me to thinking of the many references to dew in the Bible. I made a mental note to check my concordance to see just how many there were. I later found twenty-two.

There is one familiar passage (Judges 6-7) concerning dew that has special meaning for me. During the period of the Judges, Israel was being raided regularly by their neighbors, the Midianites. These strong, warlike hordes came upon Israel every harvest time, stripping the land of all the produce. *"And Israel was greatly impoverished because of the Midianites; and the children of Israel cried unto the Lord."* (Judges 6:6)

God heard the cries of His people and sent an angel to Gideon, son of Joash, and told him that He would deliver His people from the Midianites by the hand of Gideon. Like many of us, who have felt God's call to a ministry, Gideon had difficulty believing that he could be chosen for such a task. He asked for a sign, so he could be sure. The angel gave him a sign as, at his touch, the offering Gideon provided was consumed by fire. Gideon needed and asked for even more evidence of his call. He laid out a fleece and asked God to confirm his call by letting dew fall only on the fleece, while none fell anywhere else. The next morning all was dry except the fleece, which was soaked. Gideon still wasn't satisfied; and, apologizing, asked for one more test. This time let the fleece be dry while all else would be wet with dew. Again, God affirmed His call of Gideon; and Gideon, convinced he was in the will of God, went on to lead his people to a great victory, to the glory of God.

As I pondered this, I remembered vividly the time when I, too, needed God's affirmation of my call to the preaching ministry; when I, too, figuratively "laid out the fleece." I was in my fourth year of a teaching career, the fulfillment of a lifetime ambition. I was also active in every phase of the work of our church; but more and more and stronger and stronger, I felt that God wanted me to serve Him in the full time ministry. I hesitated to make the commitment, afraid that I might be mistaken, might not have heard God aright. I wanted to be certain. Finally I could hold out no longer, and I made a public commitment to the ministry. The next morning I went to my school superintendent and told him what I had done and that I wouldn't be teaching the following year. This was an act of faith because I had a wife and four children to support.

Shortly after I made my commitment, a rural church nearby called me to be their pastor. I accepted, and the Lord blessed our work there. The church grew, and several souls were saved in a revival meeting. My home church called a council of the ordained men of the Association who, after examining me as to the reality of my call and my fitness for the ministry, laid their hands on me and "set me aside" for the ministry.

About a year later, I was called to serve as pastor of a new mission church, sponsored by one of the strong churches of our Association. We began the mission with a revival meeting with me as the evangelist. Attendance at the services was good, and interest was high; but after a week of services no one had come forward to make a profession of faith. This had been true through my work thus far. I had led some to Christ in personal witnessing. Several had made professions of faith in response to the invitation, but always when someone else had preached. I became very despondent and began to question the reality of my call. I prayed and prayed, but to no avail. Finally, one sleepless night, I told God of my doubts and asked for His affirmation. I said, "Lord, tonight, let someone respond to my invitation. If someone comes to trust Christ, then I will know that I am in your will. Lord, if no one comes tonight, I will take that to mean that I was mistaken. God, I'm not doubting you, only myself. I want to be sure that I'm truly where you want me to be."

No one knew what I had done, not even my wife. I went to the service that evening with great trepidation. Realizing that this was probably the most important sermon I would ever preach, and that it may be the last one, I leaned heavily on my Lord for strength and guidance. When I finished my message and gave the invitation, the congregation began to sing the invitation hymn. I was almost afraid to look, but Praise the Lord, I saw a teen-age girl step out into the aisle and come forward. I went to meet her and heard her tearful confession of faith in Christ. I will never forget Millie Radiford, who that night gave her heart and life to Christ. Perhaps she will never know until eternity how God used her to affirm my call to the ministry that has spanned half a century.

Thank you, God, for your patient understanding of your children and your willingness to give us the assurance we need when we ask in sincerity. Amen.

16

"The pines would stand straight and tall…reaching to the sky."

FROM TRASH HEAP TO TEMPLE

A controversial practice that has been growing throughout the Ozarks, and indeed throughout the nation, is that of clear-cutting timber tracts. In this operation, everything within an area is cut. That which is marketable is utilized, and the rest is left to decay. The theory is that through natural processes a new crop of timber will spring up to eventually grow into valuable timber. The immediate result, however, is an ugly scar on the land covered by stumps, briars, sprouts and shrubs.

Near one of the paths I sometimes walk, there is such an area. As I walked through this, I often felt revulsion at what I considered the ugly track of man on the land. As I sat resting at the edge of this slashing, I began to mentally chart the processes that would make this tract into a forest again. First, after a clear cutting, would spring up grasses, weeds, and briars. Sprouts of hardwoods would then rise from the old roots and stumps, as well as seedlings from acorns left from the trees that had been removed, or scattered by birds and small animals. These deciduous sprouts would grow into saplings, eventually shading out the briars, weeds and grasses. The strongest of these would survive and thrive, while the weaker ones would eventually be eliminated. After many decades, the slow-growing hardwoods would become trees and perhaps in a century this could finally be called a forest again.

As I pondered the subject, my attention was drawn to something else that I had not noticed before. Throughout the area, almost hidden in the grasses and weeds, were small pine seedlings. Had they been planted there? But, no, there on the fringe of the surrounding woods was an occasional cone-bearing pine seed tree, *mother trees*, I had heard them called. These had provided the seeds, scattered by natures own processes.

Now, I realized another factor was added to the recovery process. The pines, faster growing than hardwoods, would soon push their tops above their neighbors, and eventually the shrubs and underbrush would also lose the struggle for light and life.

Closing my eyes, I tried to visualize what this clearing would look like in a few decades when nature had had a chance to have its way. The pines would stand straight and tall. The foliage, forming a close canopy, would shade out all undergrowth, so that the forest floor would be clear and clean except for a brown, springy carpet of pine needles. The weaker pines, even the lower branches of the strong ones, would die and decay, so there would be only the tall, straight trunks reaching to the sky like the beautiful Doric pillars left us by the ancient Greeks, to be copied by modern man in his more imposing buildings. The sunlight, filtering through the canopy of foliage would make of the forest floor a mosaic of sunlight and shadow to rival those of the great cathedrals of Europe. The wind through the foliage would produce music ranging several octaves from the deepest basses of a cathedral organ to the highest sopranos in a cathedral choir singing a great oratorio.

I thought how often I was forced to use "cathedral" to describe such a forest. How apt an allusion! How often in such a forest I had been moved with awe and reverence at the consciousness of the presence and majesty of God. Truly, such a forest is a cathedral.

Again, I looked at the clear-cut tract, but this time from a different perspective. Now I saw it, not as a site of destruction, but as a construction site. Here, God was building a cathedral to His glory and man's blessing.

How like life! So often, a life is scarred and ugly by man's rapacious misuse and wasting of his resources. Weeds and briars may run riot there and turn it into a wasteland. However, if God is allowed to have His way, He will bring order out of the chaos, turn the waste into worth, and the base into beauty. Yes, God is in the building and rebuilding business. From the life that has crashed, He can build a cathedral.

For this very reason, make
every effort to add to your
faith goodness; and to
goodness, knowledge, and to
knowledge, self-control; and
to self-control, perseverance;
and to perseverance,
godliness; and to godliness,
brotherly kindness; and to
brotherly kindness, love.
2 Peter 1:5-7 niv

17

God cares for all His creatures, even the smallest of birds; not one of them falls without His knowledge and permissive will. We are more valuable to Him than birds.

GOD, SPARROWS, AND ME

"You are worth more than many sparrows."
Matthew 10:31

One day as I walked, my attention was drawn to a bright blue object beside the trail ahead. Curious, I walked to it and found that it was the dead body of a Blue Jay. Thinking that it had been shot, or had become the prey of a predator, I examined it, finding no sign of any injury. It had evidently died of natural causes and fallen beside the trail.

The Gospel of Matthew (Matthew 10:29,31 NIV) records how Jesus said, *"Aren't two sparrows sold for only a penny? But your Father knows when any one of them falls to the ground. So don't be afraid! You are worth more than many sparrows."* Again He said: *"Look at the birds of the sky! They don't plant or harvest. They don't even store grain in barns. Yet your Father in heaven takes care of them. Aren't you worth more than birds?"* (Matthew 7:26 NIV)

As I reflected on these truths, I went on my way rejoicing in the assurance that I, too, am under the loving watch care of our heavenly Father, and that he who cares for the lowliest of birds will surely care for me.

Years later I had the opportunity to share this lesson with my little four-year-old great-granddaughter, Julianne. We were standing at our patio door, watching the birds coming and going at our feeder. Suddenly, one flew directly into the glass doors and fell to the patio. Julianne began to cry for Gee-Gee-Pa to "Help it." I picked up the bird, but saw that it was no use. It quivered a little and was dead. Julianne was devastated. It was the first time she had seen anything die. I read the verses from Matthew's Gospel to her; and we talked about their meaning and promise to us. I went to my shop and made a little wooden box. She gently wrapped the bird in one of her doll's blankets and placed it in the box. We closed the lid and buried it near our back fence. I said a little eulogy about the "nice little bird," and Julianne joined me in singing her favorite hymn, "Jesus Loves Me," changing the "me" to "you" and "ones" to birds.

"Jesus loves you; this I know,
For the Bible tells me so.
Little birds to Him belong;

They are weak, but He is strong.
Yes, Jesus loves you....[12]

We prayed, asking God to keep the nice little bird in His care, and thanking Him for caring for us. At Julianne's insistence, I made a wooden cross and set it at the head of the grave. After six years, it still marks the grave; and Julianne often picks whatever flowers are available and places them on the grave. Now at the age of ten, she still remembers and can share the lesson we learned that day. God cares for all His creatures, even the smallest of birds; and not one of them falls without His knowledge and permissive will. Since we are of more importance to Him than birds, He surely cares and provides for us.

Jesus loves me, this I know,
For the Bible tells me so....[13]

18

"As the hart panteth after the little water brooks, so my soul panteth after thee, O God." Psalm 42:1

MY SOUL THIRSTETH AFTER THEE, O GOD

I had heard hounds running in the distance one morning as I walked my solitary trail, and wondered what wild creature they were pursuing. Likely a fox, a bobcat, or a coyote, I told myself.

The hounds were far from my thoughts, however, as I found a place to sit and rest on a ledge overlooking a quiet pool in the little brook that parallels the trail for a way. The day was warm and having hiked briskly for a while, a brief respite was most welcome.

Entranced by the beauty of the scene and engrossed in my musings, my attention was attracted by a rattle of stones. A deer had appeared from the woods and was standing near the pool. He looked nervously behind him at his back trail, and his nose twitched as he tested the air for the scent of danger. His sides heaved, and his nostrils flared a little as he panted from the rigors of the chase.

A moment he stood there before he waded into the pool, thrust his muzzle into the cool water, and drank thirstily. Alternately, he lowered his head, drank quickly, and nervously raised his head to check his surroundings for some threat to his safety. A vagrant breeze must have carried my scent to him, because he was suddenly galvanized into action. His white flag raised, and with a single bound, he cleared the brook. In a split second, he disappeared from sight. Disappointed by his sudden disappearance, yet thrilled by his wild beauty, I sat there long, savoring the experience.

A verse of scripture from the Psalms came to mind, and I struggled to recall the words exactly. *"As the hart panteth after the water brooks, so my soul thirsteth after thee, O God, after the living God."* (Psalm 42:1) Had a scene such as the one I had just witnessed inspired that verse? Perhaps! Certainly, the Psalmist and I had shared other experiences of a more deeply spiritual nature.

I remembered the long years before I found God precious to my soul and received His Son as my Savior and Lord. How I had thirsted for Him! I recalled how I had sought to satisfy that thirst from the fountains of my own worldly devise. I had searched, almost frantically at times, for some meaning and purpose in life, some reason for my existence, some life-consuming goal to be pursued and achieved. Each search had left me as empty and unfulfilled as before. It was only when I found God, and in Him that peace and serenity of mind and heart He alone can give, that I came to realize that it was for Him my soul had thirsted for so long. In Him I found a meaning and purpose for my life.

I remember so well the testimony of Old Jess, the town drunk. The old derelict had been worthless to himself, to his family, and to society. A fine craftsman when sober, he could not hold a job nor stay out of jail because of drunkenness. As a result, his family suffered deprivation and shame. One day, however, Old Jess found peace with God through Jesus Christ, and his life was changed. For the rest of his life, Jess was always ready to give his testimony of what Christ can do for anyone who will receive Him. He loved to tell how he had thirsted for God but didn't know what it was that his soul longed for. He said that he had tried to quench that thirst with alcohol, to no avail; but in Christ his soul found satisfaction.

Jesus met a woman at Jacob's well in Samaria. She had gone from man to man in her efforts to quench the fires of lust that burned within her. But when she heard Jesus say, *"Whosoever drinketh of the water that I give him shall never thirst;"* she cried, *"Lord, give me this water that I thirst not."* (John 4:6)

A popular song today, written by Richard Blanchard, expresses so beautifully the prayer that brings eternal satisfaction to the soul's thirst for God:

> *Like the woman at the well, I was seeking*
> *For things that could not satisfy*
> *Then I heard my Savior speaking,*
> *'Draw from my well that never shall run dry.'*
> *Fill my cup, Lord. I lift it up, Lord.*
> *Come and quench this thirsting of my soul.*
> *Bread of heaven feed me till I want no more;*
> *Fill my cup, fill it up and make me whole.*[14]

Refreshed in body and spirit, and rejoicing in the living presence of Christ Jesus; I rose to continue my walk down the Taum Sauk Trail, buoyed by the assurance that "I'll never walk alone," nor my spirit

thirst again for God, for I have found Him. He is mine,
and I am His, forever and forever.

> Submit yourselves, then, to
> God. Resist the devil, and he
> will flee from you. Come
> near to God and he will come
> near to you.
> James 4:7-8 niv

19

Two species of mushrooms growing together: a morel, easily
identified and safe, and two others of an unidentified species,
unsafe.

MUSHROOMS AND TOADSTOOLS

"There is a way that seemeth right unto man, but the end thereof are the ways of death."
Proverbs 14:12

One of the rewards of tramping through the Ozark woods is the occasional discovery of edible mushrooms. We have two very delicious wild mushrooms: the morels that pop out over night in late spring and early summer, and the coral or goat's beard of late summer and early autumn. The morels are a real delicacy, but rather scarce and much sought after. The corals are good, and much more plentiful; but they are not as well known as morels.

There are many more species of wild mushrooms, some no doubt edible; but one has to be very knowledgeable about these because some of them are deadly poisonous. Most notorious of the poison species are the amanitas, commonly called "destroying angels."

I never see or even think of wild mushrooms without shuddering at the memory of a tragic accident, early in my ministry. A family that thought they were knowledgeable enough to safely gather these gifts of

95

Mother Nature had spent a day in the woods, gathering. They brought home a large collection of these fungi, confident that they were all safe to eat. Since they had so many, they shared their harvest with some friends who lived next door. Grateful, and delighted with the gift, the friends prepared and ate their share first. All who partook of them grew violently ill, and some of them died.

This tragedy touched me very deeply. My heart was broken for the family who lost loved ones because of the terrible mistake. I was even more sympathetic, if possible, for the family who made the mistake and caused the death of their friends. Although what they had done was done in all innocence, and out of a spirit of generosity, this did not lessen the terrible consequences of their mistake. As tragic as is acting on what we "think" is right in the physical realm, how much more is it in the spiritual. In Proverbs 14:12, we are warned of this very thing. *"There is a way that seemeth right unto man, but the end thereof are the ways of death."*

How many times we share some spiritual truth from God's word with another, only to have them respond: "Yes, I know it (Bible) says that, but it seems to me...." Then they go on to state their own idea of what they think is right, though it is in direct opposition to God's word and His will.

There is an old axiom that goes: "Ignorance (of the law) is no excuse." Certainly, this is true of the way of salvation. God has made it so clear in His inspired word that no one can plead ignorance as an excuse. Over and over again, in words that, as the Prophet Isaiah says (Isaiah 35:8) *"the wayfaring men, though fools, shall not err therein."* Jesus said in John 14:6: *"I am the way, the truth, and the life; no man cometh unto the Father, but by me."* Again, in John 3:3, He said: *"Except a man be born again, he cannot see the kingdom of God."* In addition, Paul spells it out in Ephesians 2:8: *"For by grace are ye saved through faith; and that not of yourselves; it is the gift of God."* On and on, His word makes it crystal clear that the one way of salvation is through faith in Jesus Christ. *"But as many as received Him, to them gave He power to become the sons of God, even to them that believe on his name.*" (John 1:12)

Dear God, forgive me for the many times I have followed the path that "seemed" to me to be right, rather than to seek to find the way that you would show me to be right. Father, help me to always be able to pray in all sincerity as Jesus taught us to pray: "Not my will, but thine be done." Amen

Be still before the Lord and
wait patiently for him;
Psalm 37:7a NIV

Rejoice in the Lord always. I will say it again: Rejoice! Let your gentleness be evident to all. The Lord is near. Do not be anxious about anything, but in everything, by prayer and petition, with thanksgiving, present your requests to God. And the peace of God, which transcends all understanding, will guard your hearts and your minds in Christ Jesus.

Philippians 4:4-7 NIV

20

"I placed my hands under His, buried my face in those precious hands and wept...."

I SAW JESUS

About twenty-seven years ago, I had been under treatment for several years for blocked arteries in my heart. In October of 1976, I was advised by my cardiologist to check into one of the three hospitals in St. Louis that performed cardiograms (now called heart catheterizations) to have a cardiogram done. If the cardiogram indicated a need, I would undergo coronary artery by-pass surgery. Of the three hospitals that did this surgery, I chose to go to the Jewish Hospital. Therefore, on October 19, I checked in there, into the care of cardiologist Doctor Crone. The cardiogram was done the next day, and because my condition was so critical, I was kept in intensive care until Monday, when I underwent surgery. I was given a shot about midnight Sunday that put me "out," and I did not regain consciousness until about noon on Tuesday.

When I regained consciousness, I was told about the procedures they had done. I'll not describe the gruesome details of the surgery as it was done in those days, except to say a vein was stripped from my right leg for the grafts. I was connected to a heart-lung machine and my heart and breathing was stopped. The machine did these for me. My chest was opened, and the bypasses were attached. The machine was turned off; my heart was restarted; and my chest was closed. I was then taken to the SICU recovery room, but I was hemorrhaging profusely. One of the bypasses had ripped where it was attached to my aorta. I was given whole blood transfusions as fast as it could be given, but I was losing it faster than I was getting it. I later learned that I was given twenty-one units of whole blood; and, when no more O-negative blood could be obtained, one unit of plasma. I was taken back to the operating room, put back on the heart-lung machine, my chest reopened, and the rip at my aorta was repaired. My chest was closed again, and I was returned to the recovery room in SICU.

For two days I seemed to be progressing well, but on the third day, I suddenly went into ventricular fibrillation. A "Code Blue" was called; doctors and nurses came from everywhere, and many heroic efforts to save my life were done. Finally, electric shock defibrillators were used. I was fully conscious when the paddles were placed on my chest, and I was hit by a jolt of electricity. The first jolt failed to be effective, so another, higher voltage bolt was used, this time jolting my heart into a more normal rhythm.

This whole scenario was repeated three times in the next three days. The last one happened on Sunday night. I was unconscious the whole time, some four hours. Later, I was told, by my doctors, what happened. To be brief, he said, in effect, "We lost you for a time." I, of course, knew nothing of what had transpired during that time except what I was later told, and WHAT I EXPERIENCED. It is this experience that I will share with you here.

I make no claims about this experience. I do not attach any name to it. However you wish to characterize it is your privilege. I only relate to you what I experienced during that critical time when, to use the doctor's words, 'they lost me for a time.' I know that my body never left that room in the Coronary Surgery Intensive Care Unit. It was there, being feverishly worked on by that team of doctors. I was somewhere else, moving through space, up and out, like a plane climbing on course. I wasn't conscious of any body, perhaps I had one, as I will explain later, but it certainly wasn't the one the doctors were working on. There was absolute quiet, and peace and calm. I have never known such peace and calm as I felt during that ascent. There was not one thing to disturb my mind— no fear, no concern, nor even a question of why I was there or where I was going. Just beautiful, wonderful peace and calm.

This seemed to go on for quite some time. Finally, I could see ahead of me a patch of blue, the most beautiful blue I have ever seen. It was like a beautiful blue cloud, or a huge blue drapery. As I drew nearer, it was drawn back like a stage curtain being drawn, or a cloud being rolled back and Jesus was standing there in the opening. I knew him immediately. Don't ask me how. I just knew him. I have been asked to describe him. I can't. "Did he look like the artists have painted him?" some ask. I have to answer, "I don't know." That didn't register. I just KNEW HIM! That was enough!

As I drew nearer, he came to meet me, with his hands held out before him about waist high, palms upward. I went to meet him, and now I was conscious of some kind of a body. I placed my hands under his, buried my face in his hands, and wept. My tears flowed until his hands were wet, and the tears ran through his hands, wet my hands, and ran between my fingers. It has been twenty-seven years since, but when I think about it, I can still feel those tears running between my fingers; it was so real.

Jesus was speaking to me, but it wasn't like I would speak to you. I can't explain that, but he was saying to me, "It's all right, Son. It's all right." He didn't say what was "all right," and I didn't ask. I was completely satisfied. Everything was all right.

I don't remember taking my leave. I had to come back. I know that. He wasn't through with me down here. I do remember the journey back, just like the one going out except in reverse. This time, however, I felt an urgency to get back so I could tell my dear wife, Eva, "Honey, you can stop worrying now. I saw Jesus, and he said it is all right." She was there by my bedside when I began to regain consciousness, and she says that those words were just tumbling from my lips before I was fully awake. And it is all right! Twenty-seven eventful, fruitful years have passed. I am now well past four-score years in age. My doctors tell me there isn't much else they can do for my heart. I know that my remaining time here on earth is growing short. That isn't a morbid thought, just reality; but that is all right, too. I have been there, and I can testify that for one, whose soul is anchored in Jesus, death is no threat. It is not to be feared nor dreaded.

For a long time I wondered why I wept so with my face in those precious hands. With time, I have come to understand what I think was the reason for my tears. The passage of scripture I turn to most is not one of those beautiful passages in John's Gospel. It is not in the great passages in Paul's Roman Letter. It is a few verses written by the Prophet Isaiah some seven hundred years before Jesus' birth. My Bible falls open there when it is allowed to fall open where it will, and the page is tear stained. It reads:

> *But he was pierced for our (my) transgressions, he was crushed for our (my) iniquities; the*

punishment that brought us (me) peace was upon him, and by his wounds we (I) are (am) healed. We all, like sheep, have gone astray, each of us has turned to his own way; and the Lord has laid on him the iniquity of us all. (Isaiah 53:5-6 NIV)

When I read this passage, in my mind's eye I can see a rugged cross on a rocky Judean hill, and my Saviour hanging there, suspended by iron spikes driven through his hands and feet. His back is lacerated and gouged by the lashes of the notorious Roman cat-o-nine-tails. His brow is gouged and bloody from the cruel crown of thorns placed on him in mockery, and his beard is matted with the dried mucous his tormentors had spit there. I know that he was there, bearing my sins, suffering my just punishment, dying for me! That is why I wept those many tears which wet his nail pierced hands, because my sins had nailed him, who was without sin, to the cross.

21

"God had graciously answered my prayer and sent a
guardian angel to spread his watch care over us…"

UNSEEN ANGELS

"....some have entertained angels unawares."
Hebrews 13:2

You don't have to see an angel to know that one has been with you. My wife, Eva, and I were unaware of one's presence until he took over and saved us from disaster.

On December 31, 1990, we drove from our home in Ironton to Kennett, some 135 miles south, in the Missouri "bootheel." My four older sisters and members of our extended families gathered there each New Year's Eve for a family reunion and Watch Party. There were always lots of good food, fun, and joyous fellowship.

This year was no different. We ate, played, and visited throughout the evening. As midnight approached we gathered in a big circle and sang some hymns. I was asked to lead in prayer. I thanked God for His many blessings upon us through the past year, for bringing us together for this happy occasion, and asked Him to watch over us and bless us throughout the year just beginning. I closed my prayer by asking for His watch-care over us as we traveled the highways that day and for Him to give us safe journeys home. None of us could have imagined how dramatically God would answer that prayer!

After a few short hours of sleep and a hearty breakfast, Eva and I started our drive home. As usual I drove while Eva slept. After about two hours, I had become so sleepy that I realized it was unsafe for me to drive further. About twenty miles south of Fredericktown, I pulled over and stopped. I asked Eva if she thought she was awake and rested enough to drive the remaining thirty-five miles home. She said she would try. Exchanging places, she began to drive, and I fell instantly asleep.

Highway 67 bypasses Fredericktown on the west. About a quarter mile south of our exit to route 72, where we turned west to Ironton, 67 becomes a four-lane divided highway.

I was soundly asleep and unaware that Eva, overcome by fatigue and lack of sleep, had been lulled into a virtual trance-like stupor. As we approached the dividing lanes, I was suddenly, inexplicably wide-awake. Eva, as though mesmerized, was going straight ahead into the southbound lanes, heading directly toward an oncoming vehicle. A collision was imminent! My left hand moved, seemingly of its own accord, grasped the steering wheel, and against Eva's frozen grip on it, swung the car to the right, across the beginning of the median, into the northbound lanes, and then onto the wide, paved shoulder. Eva, shocked out of her stupor, braked us to a stop.

Shifting into park and turning off the ignition, she gasped, "What happened?"

"I don't know," I answered. "Something— someone—woke me up. We were heading into the wrong-way lanes. I grabbed the wheel and turned us back, just in time. At least I guess I did. It was very close."

"I don't see how you could have done it –wake up, grasp what was happening, and react so quickly," Eva said.

Then the realization hit me. "I didn't. I couldn't have," I answered.

There could be only one answer, I knew. Someone else was riding with us, had wakened me, had used my arm and hand and his strength to save us from disaster. God had graciously answered my prayer and sent a guardian angel to spread his watch care over us and give us our safe journey home.

> Praise be to the Lord, to God our Savior, who daily bears our burdens.
> Psalms 68:19 NIV

Let us hold unswervingly to the hope we profess, for he who promised is faithful.

Hebrews 10:23 NIV

22

"Among the many rewards such nature walks provide is the abundance and variety of butterflies that gladden the eye."

BVTTERFLIES, SYMBOL OF THE RESVRRECTION

"For the invisible things of him from the creation of the world are clearly seen, being understood by the things that are made, even His eternal power and Godhead...." Romans 1:20

If one spends much time in the outdoors, especially in areas untouched by the despoiling hands of man, and has a heart and mind open to God's revelation of Himself, he will come to know God and His eternal power as never before. Among the many rewards such nature walks provide is the abundance and variety of butterflies that gladden the eye. A lepidopterist's guidebook will help one to identify and record the many different species seen, so they can be 'collected' and claimed as ones own without harming them in any way.

One day I had been especially gladdened by seeing several of these lovely insects and reflected on the lessons they teach so beautifully. I remembered a time when I was asked to visit a school class just before Easter and speak to the children on the meaning of the event. Holding the attention of third-graders is difficult at best, so it was with trepidation that I agreed, and made preparation.

I decided to use the 'chalk-talk' approach. Using sheets of newsprint and colored chalk, I first drew a picture of a loathsome caterpillar. The pupils, especially the boys, related to that. Then on the second sheet, I drew a picture of a chrysalis and explained how the caterpillar, when the time was right, spun the shell about itself and waited. Some child asked the question that no doubt was on the mind of the rest of the class: "Waited for what?" I then quickly sketched on the third sheet a picture of a beautiful butterfly and explained that when the time was right, the caterpillar would burst its shell and come out, no longer an ugly caterpillar, but now a beautiful butterfly.

Building on this, I told the story of the resurrection and led them to see why the butterfly was a fitting reminder of the reality of the resurrection. I went on then to speak of the promise of our own resurrection. Just as the caterpillar bursts forth from the chrysalis to a new life, God has promised that those who are dead in Christ will come forth from the grave, not in the old, corrupt body, but in a new body in the image of Christ.

Thank you, Father, for the beautiful truths you reveal to us through the things you have made. Thank you for the reminder of the resurrection of our Lord Jesus through the life cycle of the beautiful butterflies. Thank you, Father, for their reminder that we, too, may be "born again," a new creature in Christ Jesus. Thank you, God, for the beauty of your creation that gladdens the eyes of the beholder. Amen.

Blessed is the man who perseveres under trial, because he as stood the test, he will receive the crown of life that God has promised to those who love him..

James 1:12 niv

23

The three-room school building in Wappapello, Missouri, where I attended my seventh, eighth, ninth, and tenth grades in school. Here hate was born in me that endured for sixty years.

FREE AT LAST

In the late summer of 1934, I started my eighth grade in school. Our school in the village of Wappapello, Missouri consisted of three rooms: first through fourth in one, fifth through eighth in another, and ninth and tenth in the third. Our middle-grade teacher, Hugh Floyd (not his real name), was new to our school. He was a big, strapping young man then, a dedicated teacher and stern disciplinarian. He was firmly determined to establish control over what had been an unruly class.

A few weeks into the term, I was one of four involved in a minor infraction of the rules, and the first to be disciplined by being whipped with a seasoned hickory sprout. Perhaps influenced by the story of the Spartan lad who had endured without flinching while a kit fox hidden in his clothing gnawed at his vitals, I never flinched, cried, nor showed any sign of pain as he laid on the blows. Evidently because of my stoicism, Mr. Floyd was unaware of the severity of the beating he gave me. When it was over, my legs from my hips to my ankles were covered by a crisscross of red welts as

119

large as one's finger that became black stripes that lasted for weeks. I was left with a burning hatred for the man, and a determination to, someday, get revenge for the beating. I carried that grudge inside me for years, often recounting that experience to others, and describing how I would return the beating, someday.

Time passed, slowly for a youth, but swiftly in retrospect. On one memorable day, Sunday, June 15, 1941, two life-changing events occurred. At nine o'clock that Sunday morning, I married my high-school sweetheart; and at the close of the morning worship service, I accepted Jesus Christ as my Lord and Savior. I wish that I could say that the long held hatred and grudge was repented of and taken away. It wasn't. Rather, it was just hidden away and never allowed to surface.

Many eventful years followed; war-time service in the Army Air Corps, college education, career as a school teacher, surrender to God's call to the gospel ministry, theological seminary study followed by pastoral ministry, all the while providing, and rearing and educating our four children. The grudge I held, though, was still there, buried in my subconscious and never brought out and dealt with.

In 1994, now seventy-two years old and retired, I was asked to deliver the morning message at the annual homecoming at Lowndes, Missouri. In preparing to speak, I prayed earnestly that God would guide me in my message, speaking through me just the words that someone in the congregation needed to hear. How wonderfully God answered my prayer! How surprising, that I was the one to whom He would speak.

When I arrived at the church where the service was to be held, I started to sign the visitor's register. As I glanced down the column of names, one caught my eye, Hugh Floyd! After nearly sixty years I would come face to face with the man I had hated so long.

The service was ready to begin; so I took my place on the rostrum. I asked the chairman about Mr. Floyd, and he pointed him out to me. As I looked out at the old man, now in his late eighties, I was filled with a feeling far different than I had expected. Instead of hatred, I felt a surge of compassion; and the old anger was replaced with love. When I stood to speak, my carefully prepared speech was abandoned, and I read the "Lord's Prayer" from "The Sermon on the Mount" (Matthew 6:9-15). I spoke from my heart of forgiveness, with emphasis on Jesus' words in verse fifteen: *"But if ye forgive not men their trespasses, neither will your Father forgive your trespasses."*

Then it was that I realized how God had answered my prayer through my own lips with the words that I needed to hear.

As soon as the service ended, I hurried to the man I had vowed to wreak vengeance upon and introduced myself.

To my amazement, he said, "Oh, yes, I remember you, Ed. You were always the last to be standing in our spelling and ciphering matches."

I put my arms around the old man and told him how I had held a grudge against him, but that God had taken it all away. I asked him to forgive me, and told him that I loved him as God had loved and forgiven me. In that moment I felt a burden lifted from my heart, and a feeling of wholeness engulfed me. Truly free, I at last could know all *the "peace of God which passeth all understanding..."* (Philippians 4:7)

Be joyful always continuously; give thanks in all circumstances, for this is God's will for you in Christ Jesus.
1 Thessalonians 5:16-18 niv

24

The United Methodist Church at Lowndes, Missouri, where my mother professed her faith in Christ over 100 years ago, where I attended Sunday School as a pre-teen, and where I, delivering the Homecoming address in 1994, was finally set free from a sixty-four year old animosity.

For it is by grace you have been saved, through faith--- and this not from yourselves, it is the gift of God---not by works, so that no one can boast.

Ephesians 2:8-9 NIV

25

The First Baptist Church, Senath, Missouri.
"Poor indeed is the person who doesn't have some place so
meaningful, so fraught with precious memories, so
influential in his life that it becomes almost a shrine..."

MY TRIBUTE TO THE FIRST BAPTIST CHURCH OF SENATH - 1986

Poor indeed is the person who does not have some place so meaningful, so fraught with precious memories, so influential in his life that it becomes almost a shrine, a place so holy that to go there is to feel the very Shekinah presence and Doxa glory of God. The First Baptist Church of Senath is that special place for me. There are many reasons why.

It was here in this holy place that I trusted Christ Jesus as my Savior and was born again, a new creation. It was on my wedding day, June 15, 1941. The church was in revival, led by Rev. Jeff Rousseau and the pastor, Rev. R. F. Liddell. My wife-to-be, Eva Hipps, had taken me to the revival services every evening that week, and I was under deep conviction. I felt the Lord's presence very powerfully at each service. Every hymn sung and every word of every sermon seemed to be for me and me alone.

Eva and I were married by the pastor early on Sunday morning. After the ceremony, both Rev.

Liddell and Rev. Rousseau again laid God's claim on my heart. Later that morning, when the invitation was given at the close of the morning service, I surrendered my heart and will to Christ and confessed Him as my Savior and Lord. In the words of the song, "Heaven came down and glory filled my soul." My burden was lifted, and God's peace flooded my heart and soul. Ever since, this place has been my "Bethel," for like Jacob, here I met God and entered into the Covenant with Him. To me, this truly is "Beth-el," the house of God.

This place is special to me, too, for the part it had in my courtship and marriage to my wife and companion of over forty-five years. Although it was at school, not the church, that I met Eva, the church was central during the months of our courtship and subsequent marriage. The church, its pastors, and members had been influential in Eva's life. Here she had been taught and led to Christ. Here she had been baptized and led to grow in grace and knowledge of God and His Word. It was here, that she brought me so often during those months of courtship. Here I learned what a church really was and of the ties of love that bound it together. It was no wonder that here, on the day our lives were united in marriage that I also found Christ and united with the church.

Shortly after our marriage, we left Senath for work in the city. There, no one cared for our spiritual well being, and without the church I did not grow as a Christian. Some years of changing jobs and residence, wartime service in the Air Force, and the readjustments after discharge allowed me to drift further and further from the Lord. However, the Lord never gave up on me; and through His chastisement and loving conviction, I eventually was led back to Him. Again, the Senath Church was central in that reunion. After weeks of agony and soul-searching, I came to the church and found the pastor, Rev. Bob Braden, behind the church in bib overalls, leading some Vacation Bible School boys in handcraft projects. Under the big oak tree that stood between the church and annex, I unburdened my heart and was led gently and lovingly to repentance and rededication of my life to Christ. Later, I made that renewal public at the altar, and the membership showered me with their love and affirmation. Again, that glowing presence of God in this place was made real. Like Jacob on the shore of the brook Jabbok, I had wrestled with God here, settled my account with Him, and received His blessing. Ever since, this has been my own special Penuel.

This church is special too in the part it played in my growth as a Christian. Through the Church, here I came to grips with the demands of stewardship. The church taught me that the tithe is the Lord's and the beginning of good stewardship. Here I committed myself to tithing and learned that God's laws of economics transcend man's understanding. I learned that one can never out-give God. With this further victory, God again blessed me here in this holy place.

Here I first served in a church organization when I was enlisted in Training Union by some dear old saints: Mrs. Douglas, Mrs. Via, Mrs. White, Mrs. Utley and others. I was in my mid-twenties and the only man in that union composed mostly of elderly widows. They elected me as Bible Quiz Leader, and I became a daily reader of God's blessed Word.

Here I taught my first Sunday School class when I was asked to be a substitute for Brother Virgil O'Connor's class. Here I was elected Associate Sunday School Superintendent with Brother Buddy Douglas and had to fill in when he had extensive dental work. Here I led in public prayer for the first time. It was here also, that I learned the joy and thrill of leading a precious soul to salvation in Jesus Christ. In all this, it was the church that nourished and nurtured me, and helped me to grow toward spiritual maturity.

For Paul the Apostle, there was a spot on the Damascus Road that would be forever hallowed ground, for there he met Jesus face to face and received his call to his great ministry. I don't know if Paul ever visited that spot in the flesh, but he went there often in memory. In his preaching and writing, Paul would often say, "let me tell you what happened to me on the Damascus Road," and he would relate his experience of salvation, his call, and his surrender. There he at last said, "Lord, what will you have me to do?" The Senath Church is my own Damascus Road, for here I also heard the Lord calling me to a special service; and here

I surrendered to what He would have me to do. During that struggle to know the Lord's will, I counseled often with the pastor, Rev. Bob Braden and retired pastor, Rev. R. F. Liddell. They were both present when I finally ceased to 'kick against the pricks' and committed my life to the gospel ministry. Again, like at my conversion and my rededication, this holy place was filled with the presence and glory of God. It has for me the same holy significance and meaning as that place in the temple where Isaiah *"saw the Lord sitting upon a throne, high and lifted up..."* (Isaiah 6:1) and heard Him say: *"Whom shall I send, and who will go for us?"* Like Isaiah, I answered, "Here am I, Lord; send me." (Isaiah 6:8)

It was the Senath Church that called together a council of the ordained men of Black River Association to consider my ordination to the gospel ministry. Here, after examination by the council and their recommendation, the Church affirmed my call and voted to proceed with my ordination. It was here at the altar I knelt while these men of God laid their hands on me and lifted me and my ministry to God in their

132

prayers. No words can ever describe, nor any mortal ever comprehend, what I felt as I knelt there in that service. But that place shall ever be a holy and sacred place for me, my **BETHEL,** my **PENUEL,** my **DAMASCUS ROAD,** and my own **TEMPLE.** Here I can go again and again, in the flesh or in spirit, and feel again the Shekinah presence and the Doxa glory of God.

What does the First Baptist Church of Senath mean to me? It is my spiritual mother. It is my touchstone of the spirit. It is the nearest to a holy shrine that I have in this world. It is the object of my most earnest prayers for its progress and prosperity as it began its second century of ministry, and until the Lord Himself comes to rapture her. AMEN.

26

My Mother and Father, with their soldier son.
My Homecoming was so sweet, and so sad.

HOMECOMINGS

".... man goeth to his long home...." Ecclesiastes 12:5

Having been a teacher for nineteen years, I am invited to many class reunions, most of them in connection with school "Homecomings." In addition, after fifty years pastoral ministry in several churches, I am often asked to participate in church homecoming events. On one particular morning, I was dealing with a dilemma, an invitation to two such homecomings on the same date. As I walked my familiar trail, my mind was filled with the subject of homecoming.

The Bible is filled with accounts of those who "came home." One familiar one is found in the book of Ruth. Naomi, her husband, and two sons had been driven by famine from their home in Judah to refuge in Moab. Her husband died there, and her sons married women of Moab. When her sons also died, Naomi decided to return home to Judah. When her daughters-in-law tried to go with her, she admonished them to stay in their homeland. One of them did; but the other, Ruth, refused to stay, but went with Naomi to Judah.

When they arrived in Bethlehem, Naomi was greeted joyously by the people. Naomi, however, said, *"Call me not Naomi, call met Mara* (bitter)...*I went out full, and the Lord hath brought me home again empty."* (Ruth 1:20-21)

As I read this, I realize that Naomi, without intending to, stated a great truth. Taking part of her statement out of context, it could read: *"...the Lord hath brought me home...."* Whether they be Bible homecomings, or our own homecomings, this is literally true. The Lord often brings us home!

Consider that familiar story of the "Prodigal Son" in Luke, chapter fifteen. Was it not the Lord who sent the wayward son, broken and repentant, back home to the loving and waiting arms of his father? How many times in each of our lives has the Lord brought us home, to a happy and joyous reunion.

During World War II, I had finished my training as an Aerial Navigator, received my silver wings and commission, and a graduation leave. My mother, though in precarious health, was so anxious to see her son that she insisted on accompanying my father on the forty-mile drive to meet the train that was bringing me home. It was a joyous and happy occasion. We had a week together before she suffered a heart attack and died three days later. I was crushed, but God gave me peace and enabled me to rejoice that I had that happy homecoming and the week with my mother before she was called to her heavenly home.

Later, when the terrible war was ended, I completed my enlistment and was eligible to be discharged. Leaving my base in California, I traveled by train the over two thousand miles back to my home, my darling wife, and our two precious daughters. The rhythmic clicking of the train wheels on the rails seemed to sing the song that was in my heart: "Going Home, Going Home, Going Home."

As sweet as these literal homecomings are, there are others just as precious, our spiritual homecomings. I was nineteen years old, a wayward child, when Christ spoke to my heart and called me from my wilderness of sin to come home to him. I don't remember what invitation song the congregation was singing that morning, but its message to my heart is summed up in the words of another hymn: *"Earnestly, tenderly, Jesus is calling, calling, 'O Sinner, come home'."*[16] What a joyous happy homecoming that was, when I turned my back on my sinful life and "came home" to Jesus.

All of us can relate to the message of another great hymn: *"....Prone to wander, Lord, I feel it; prone to leave the God I love...."*[17] Oh, how prone we are to let the world lure us, to crowd God out, and lead us astray. Who of us has not heard God speaking to our heart through another beloved hymn of invitation:

"I've wandered far away from God,
Now I'm coming home;
The paths of sin too long I've trod,.
Lord, I'm coming home.
Coming home. coming home.
Nevermore to roam;
Open wide thine arms of love,
Lord, I'm coming home."[18]

As my thoughts continued on the subject of homecomings, I remembered another related passage in Ecclesiastes 12:5, which speaks of death, but in terms that are neither morbid nor forbidding: *"...man goeth to his long home."* What a beautiful thought that is. One in the right relation with God is destined to go and for eternity, to his heavenly home—his LONG home. I have sat beside the bed of many over the years as they left the bondage of their earthly bodies and took their flight to their heavenly home. I have seen the smiles on some lips. I have heard some call the names of loved ones that had gone on before. Those were blessed moments for I could almost see the happy, joyous reunions taking place in that "long home" that Jesus, speaking to the repentant, believing thief on the cross, called PARADISE.

So I will go on, attending some homecomings here, remembering homecomings of the past, and anticipating that time when God will call me to come to my own "Long Home," with Him.

27

Taum Sauk Lake nestles serenely amid the hardwood covered hills, ablaze with their autumn foliage.

THROUGH THE VALLEY OF SHADOWS

I had tarried late on my walk. As I trudged along, forcing my protesting body to the limit of endurance, my path emerged into one of the rocky glades so typical of my beloved Ozark hills. The westering sun still bathed the mountaintops with sufficient light to follow easily the well-defined trail, but the valleys were already shrouded in deep shadows.

As I rested there on the mountaintop, I contemplated the darkened valley into which my trail plunged sharply. The shadows were grim and foreboding. I found myself wishing that somehow I could stay on the mountain and avoid descending into the darkness of the valley.

How like life, I thought. In order to tread the mountaintops, we must be prepared to walk the valleys that lie between. How exhilarating those wonderful times we spend in the sunglow of our mountain top experiences. How prone we are to echo the plea of Simon Peter the Disciple, "Lord, let us just stay here on the mountain." Yet ever the valleys beckon, and ever we must follow the descending trail.

David, the Sweet Psalmist of Israel, had trod the mountaintops with God, and his songs about them still stir the hearts of men. For every mountaintop in David's life, there was a dark, grim valley to tread. It was out of his dark valley experience, which came his best-loved psalm of faith:

> *Yea, though I walk through the valley of the shadow of death, I will fear no evil, for thou art with me."* (Psalms 23:4)

My broken health had plunged me into the dark valley, too. My way was shadowed in darkness, and my future was grim and uncertain. Even the shadows of death hung threateningly over my way. The words of an old spiritual came to me:

> *You've gotta walk that lonesome valley.*
> *You've gotta go there for yourself.*
> *There's nobody else can go there for you;*
> *You've gotta go there for yourself.*[20]

Yes, this is my dark valley, I know. No one else can walk it for me, even if there were those who would. I know that, though I walk through the valley of the shadow of death, I need fear no evil, for God is with me. Because He is with me, I will have the courage and strength to walk my valleys, ever confident that beyond the valley my trail will climb to the sunbathed heights again. Renewed in spirit, I turned again to my trail and set my face toward the valley and home.

Trust in the Lord with all your heart and lean not on your own understanding; in all your ways acknowledge him, and he will make your paths straight.
Proverbs 3:5-6 niv

28

"…we stopped at a favorite rest stop of mine,
a fallen tree or 'blow-down' in Ozark idiom."

GOD WANTS US TO KNOW

While most of my walks were solitary ones, there were those times when I chose to be accompanied by a friend. I have found that there is something about being surrounded by God's handiwork in nature that enables friends to open up and share their most personal concerns. I remember so well one of these occasions.

A friend and co-worker of mine had spoken to me about his concern for his relationship to God. He had attended Sunday School and worship services at churches in his youth, but had never made a public profession of faith in Christ, nor been baptized. Our contacts at work (teaching) never allowed much chance for in depth discussion of this nature, so I asked him to accompany me on one of my walks.

After having walked for quite some time, we stopped at a favorite rest stop of mine: a fallen tree or 'blow-down' in Ozark idiom. Seated on the old tree trunk, we spoke of the beauty of the day, and our love of the outdoors. Then, to guide the discussion in the direction I wanted, I remarked: "Bill, (not his real name) this is a beautiful old world, and it is sad to think that one day I'll have to leave it. The only thing that eases that sadness is the knowledge that I'm going to one even more beautiful."

Bill nodded. "Yes, if one could just know for sure where he was going when he leaves here."

"You can know, Bill," I answered. "God wants us to know; and, He has made it possible for us to know."

Taking my pocket Bible out, I turned quickly to the First Epistle of John and pointing to the passage, I asked him to read it. He read: *"These things have I written unto you that believe on the name of the Son of God; that ye may know that ye have eternal life, and that ye may believe on the name of the Son of God."* (1 John 5:13)

I asked, "Why does John, the Apostle of Jesus, say he had written this letter? So that believers who read it could know that they had eternal life. Doesn't that mean that one can know, Bill?"

Bill nodded, and I continued. Turning to II Timothy 1:12 and pointing to the passage, I asked him again to read, beginning at "...nevertheless..."

He read: "...*nevertheless, I am not ashamed: for I know whom I have believed, and am persuaded that he is able to keep that which I have committed unto him against that day.*"

"What did Paul say about 'knowing'?" I asked. When Bill hesitated, I added: "He said he KNEW whom he believed, and was sure he was able to keep him, didn't he, Bill?"

"Yeah, I guess so," Bill said.

"Bill," I asked, "Do you know that you have eternal life? Do you know where you will spend eternity when this life is over?"

"No, I don't know, and that's what has been bothering me," he murmured.

"The Bible says you CAN KNOW, Bill. Would you like me to show you how you can know," I asked. Then, without waiting for a reply, I again opened my Bible and turned to the book of Ephesians, chapter two. Pointing to verses eight, nine and ten, which I had highlighted and underlined, I held it for him to see. "Read this with me, Bill, I said, and began reading slowly: *"For by grace are you saved through faith; and that not of yourselves: it is the gift of God: Not of works, lest any man should boast."* (Ephesians 2:8-10)

Explaining to Bill the meaning of GRACE, received by FAITH, I emphasized Paul's statement that it was the "GIFT of God." We talked about that for a moment. Then I asked, "If I offered you a gift, what would you need to do for it to become yours, Bill?"

"Just take it, I guess," he replied.

"Right on," I said. "You don't earn a gift. You don't purchase a gift. You just receive it. Otherwise it wouldn't be a gift, would it? When does it become yours? When you accept it, just reach out and take it!"

Turning again in the Bible, this time to Romans, chapter 3, verse 23, I pointed to this, another high lighted passage, saying: "Bill, everyone of us are or were in the same predicament. See here what Paul writes: *'For all have sinned and come short of the glory of God'* (Romans 3:23). That doesn't leave anyone out, does it, Bill? All of us are sinners. I am a sinner; my wife is a sinner; and, Bill, the Bible says here that you, too, are a sinner. Isn't that right?"

Bill nodded his acknowledgement. I continued by turning a few pages over to another highlighted passage. Pointing to the first line of the verse, I asked him to read it.

He read: *"For the wages of sin is death;"* (Romans 6:23).

When he paused, I said, "Our wages are what we deserve for what we do, aren't they, Bill? The wages of sin is death, and since all of us die physically, that isn't the death this means, is it. Over in the book of Revelation 20:14, this is called The Second Death, and is described as being cast into the lake of fire or hell. So that is the predicament all of us face. But, Bill, the verse doesn't end there! Read the rest of it." He read: *"...but the gift of God is eternal life through Jesus Christ our Lord."*

"There's that word 'gift' again, Bill, " I said. "The wages of our sin is death or hell, but God, through Jesus, offers us the gift of eternal life instead. Like you

149

Turning then to Romans, chapter ten, I pointed to highlighted verses, eight through ten, and read this passage as he followed. *"But what saith it (the Bible) The word is nigh thee, even in thy mouth and in thy heart, that is the word of faith which we preach; that if thou shalt confess with thy mouth the Lord Jesus, and believe in thine heart that God hath raised him from the dead, thou shalt be saved. For with the heart man believeth unto righteousness; and with the mouth confession is made unto salvation."* Then skipping down and pointing to the thirteenth verse, I asked Bill to read. He read: *"For whosoever shall call upon the name of the Lord shall be saved."* (Romans 10:8-10, 13)

"Bill." I said gently, "You, like me and all others, have sinned; but Jesus died on the cross in our place to save us from the guilt and penalty of our sins. He offers us, offers you, Bill, the gift of forgiveness and eternal life, if you will only receive it by faith in him. You just read his promise that 'whosoever shall call upon the name of the Lord shall be saved. Bill, do you believe that promise?"

Bill nodded, and I continued: "Then will you just kneel with me here by this old fallen log and pray, asking Jesus to come into your heart and live in you, to give you that precious gift of eternal life?"

There, in the quiet of those eternal hills, Bill knelt with me, and I led him gently as he prayed the sinner's prayer. When he had finished, I prayed, and then pointed again to the promise and asked: "Bill, God's word says here that whoever calls upon the name of the Lord shall be saved. You have just called upon him. You have asked for his gift of eternal life. Now, my friend, by the authority of God's holy word, do you have eternal life? Are you now saved?"

"Oh, yes! Yes! Thank you! Thank you, Jesus!" He grabbed me in a big bear hug.

"One thing more, Bill," I said when I could get my breath. "There's another verse of scripture I want you to see, to claim as your own, and to never forget."

Turning to the Gospel of John, chapter five, verse 24, I pointed to that highlighted and underlined verse and asked him to read.

There was a joyful lilt in his voice as he read these words of Jesus: *"Verily, verily, I say unto you, he that heareth my word, and believeth on him that sent me, hath everlasting life, and shall not come into condemnation; but is passed from death unto life."* (John 5:24)

This new life you now have, Bill; how long will it last?" I asked.

"Forever and ever," he answered.

"And when will it end," I asked.

"Never," he replied.

We went on our way, refreshed and rejoicing. The following Sunday, Bill went forward in his church to make a public profession of his faith in Christ as his Savior and Lord. On the following Sunday, he was baptized.

POST SCRIPT

Bill served the Lord in his church following his baptism. About five years later, not yet having reached his fiftieth birthday, Bill died suddenly of a massive heart attack. I was deeply saddened by his death, but because of that morning when we rested by a fallen tree along the Taum Sauk Trail, I was comforted, knowing where he had gone to spend eternity.

> Every good and perfect gift is from above, coming down from the Father of the heavenly lights, who does not change like shifting shadows..
> James1:17 niv

INDEX OF SCRIPTVRES

Acts 24:24-26 59
2 Chronicles 20:26 33
2 Corinthians 1:20 50
2 Corinthians12:9 NIV 39
Ecclesiastes 12:5 .... 135, 138
Ephesians 2:8 97
Ephesians 2:8-9 125
Ephesians 2:8-10 148
Galations 2:20 NIV 29
Genesis 50:20 65
Hebrews 9:27 32
Hebrews 10:23 NIV 113
Hebrews 11:1,6 NIV 4
Hebrews 13:2 109
Isaiah 6:3 55
Isaiah 6:8 132
Isaiah 35:8 97
Isaiah 40:29-31 .... 68, 70
Isaiah 53:5-6 NIV 107
Isaiah 55:12 .... 37, 38
James 1:12 NIV 117
James 1:17 NIV 153
James 4:7-8 NIV 93
Jeremiah 1:5 54
Jeremiah 6:16 .... 40, 42
John 1:12 98
John 3:3 97
John 4:6 92
John 5:24 152
John 14:6 97
John 16:3 NIV 66
1 John 5:13 146
1 John 5:14-15 NIV 51
Jude 1:24-25 NIV 67
Judges 6:6 73
Mark 11:24 23
Matthew 6:9-15 122
Matthew 7:13-14 20

Matthew 7:26 NIV 85
Matthew 10:29,31 NIV 85
Matthew 10:31 85
Matthew 28:20 32
1 Peter 5:7 NIV 22
2 Peter 1:10 59
2 Peter 1:5-7 NIV 83
Philippians 4:4-7 .... 99, 123
Philippians 4:13 8
Proverbs 3:5-6 NIV 143
Proverbs 14:12 .... 95, 96
Psalms 8:4 53
Psalms 23:4 NIV 32, 142
Psalms 37:4 NIV 28
Psalms 37:7a 98
Psalms 42:1 .... 88, 90
Psalms 46:10 63
Psalms 51:10 NIV 8
Psalms 66:5 NIV 43
Psalms 67:1-2 NIV 47
Psalms 68:19 NIV 112
Psalms 84:56 NIV 32
Psalms 95:7-8 59
Psalms 104:10-11 .... 44, 47
Psalms 121:1 12
Revelation 20:14 149
Revelation 7:12 NIV 59
Romans 1:16 NIV 60
Romans 1:20 115
Romans 10:8-10, 13 150
Romans 3:23 148
Romans 6:23 .... 21, 149
Romans 8:26 NIV 9
Romans 8:28 .... 28, 65
Ruth 1:20-21 136
1 Thessalonians 6:16-18 NIV 123
1 Timothy 1:12 NIV 13
2 Timothy 1:12 147

REFERENCES

[1] Passage from the "Prelude of the Vision of Sir Launfel"
   by James Russell Lowell.

[2] Quoted from "Trees," by Joyce Kilmer.

[3] Quoted from "Rhodora," by Ralph Waldo Emerson.

[4] Quoted from the hymn "How Great Thou Art," by Stuart K.
   Hine

[5] Quoted from "The Rainy Day", Author Unknown

[6] Ibid

[7] Poem, "Wonder" by Edgar J. St. Clair.

[8] Quoted from hymn, "HaveThine Own Way, Lord"
   by Adelaide A. Pollard, 1862-1934

[9] Quoted from "The Roadmender," by Michael Fairless.

[10] Ibid

[11] Photo from Birds & Blooms, December/January 2002, page 15

[12] Adapted from the children's song, "Jesus Loves Me,"
   author unknown.

[13] Ibid

[14] Quoted from hymn, "Fill My Cup, Lord," by Richard Blanchard,
   1899

[15] Photo from Birds & Blooms, December/January 2002, page 41

[16] Quoted from hymn, "Jesus Is Tenderly Calling," Fannie J.
   Crosby, 1820-1915

[17] Quoted from hymn, "Come, Thou Fount of Every Blessing,"
   Robert Robinson, 1735-1790

[18] Quoted from hymn, "Lord, I'm Coming Home,"
   by William J. Kirkpatrick

[19] Photo by Glenda Powers

[20] From an old spiritual or folk song, author unknown.

ABOUT THE AUTHOR

Edgar St. Clair was born in a saw mill camp in "Smoky Hollow" in Wayne County, Missouri on April 4, 1922.

He married his high school sweetheart, Eva, June 15, 1941. In WW II he served in the Army Air Corps as a navigator. After discharge, he became a teacher. He answered the call to the Gospel Ministry in 1950, and served as a pastor until retiring in 1998.

His education included a B.S. in Education at Arkansas State College, graduating Summa Cum Laude. He earned an M.A. at Southeast Missouri State University, majoring in Counseling. His theological training was received at the Southern Baptist Seminary in Kentucky.

Ed and his wife, Eva, will soon celebrate their sixty-third wedding anniversary. They have four children, nine grandchildren, and twenty great-grandchildren. Ed fills his time attending church, preaching occasionally, reading, and writing. He has had several articles and poems published in periodicals

Printed in the United States
19376LVS00001B/70-312

9 781591 606505